Chance
Rhythm
Rhyme

ALSO BY STEVEN SWANK

The Horse Knows

Unfold

CHANCE
RHYTHM
RHYME

New Poems

2017–2019

STEVEN SWANK

FCP

Full Court Press
Englewood Cliffs, New Jersey

First Edition

Published in the United States of America
by Full Court Press, 601 Palisade Avenue,
Englewood Cliffs, NJ 07632
fullcourtpress.com

ISBN 978-1-946989-58-1
Library of Congress Control Number: 2020907203

Cover art by the author

Editing and book design by Barry Sheinkopf

To the many seeking better ideas

for justice, health, and harmony with each other
and the varied life forms on this planet,
I dedicate this book.

I delight in this opportunity to tell you what a
gift you are to the world. Though life can be
sometimes difficult, it is also fun, joyous, and worthwhile.
I have much admiration for who you are.

We are small jots in the language of the universe
yet abide in the loving consciousness of all things,
in the great stone of mountains,
in the eye of a gnat,
the energy of exploding stars.

ACKNOWLEDGMENTS

There are many reasons I write, some of which are unknowable, some subtle as the wash of moonlight, others as obvious as scented soap.

Among the many helpers I have met along the path of this volume as mentors and friends: my family, especially Daryl Goldberg.

I also thank Barry Sheinkopf (publisher of Full Court Press), Anupama Amaran (RiverRiver.org.), Juan Pablo Mobili, Siwsan Gimprich, and Jack Rosenberg. Also, and with great affection, the writers of the RiverRiver and Zee writers' groups, where many of these poems had their genesis.

TABLE OF CONTENTS

2017

2018

2019

2017

ANU NOTION OF WRITERS

She has a notion of writers—
rightly purposed, endeavored, attended—
to meet weekly in fits of composition,

the magic of willing hearts,
soulful intent, individuals
whose attention and whose hands
do the focused work of creativity.

Tune out the wash of distraction,
establish practices, endorse posture,
enrich the breath;
accepting prompts and being vulnerable
become a sumptuous gathering of friends.

ASSEMBLAGE POINT

The wants and need of the inner child
are not always the same as those of the adult.

When these are in direct conflict,
disharmonious trouble ensues.

Abraham Lincoln's comment,
"Angels of our better nature," comes to mind:

We are not enemies, but friends.
We must not be enemies.
Though passion may have strained,
it must not break our bonds of affection.
The mystic chords of memory
will swell when again touched,
as surely they will be,
by the better angels of our nature.

Recently, I had a shift
in the location of my assemblage point,
it is the focal point on our illumines sphere
that helps create our personal reality.

BECAUSE OF YOU

I hear the condenser but not the muse.
I am tired, hungry, bruised.

You cause the urge to hide, the witness to step forth:
cause me to see the richness of each moment,
to savor the unspent and unencumbered.

You cause me to cancel the agenda, toss the plan;
question my reason and my expectations,
slow the mind, quiet the breath.

Like a sneeze, an abrupt exhalation,
you startle and turn me.

Working on the roof, I burn in the sun,
wind whips colorful leaves around my head;
I live in constant danger of the fall.

BLOOD RAIN

Last night we had a blood rain.

Winds of the Sahara carry sand
up into the atmosphere
where it blows across the Atlantic
and falls here on the farm, leaving
rust-colored spots everywhere.

BUTTONS

"Buttons: from the French *bouton*, worn as ornaments as early as 2000 B.C.; early buttons made of wood, bone, metal, clay, glass, and worn as ornamentation first used with button holes in the 13th century."

Buttons often outlast their fabric
and reuse very common,
at least in our home. We have jars of them
waiting their next function, homemade clothes,
making spinners of them with string,
moving them from bowl to bowl with toes.

Candle

Unlike the opera,
candlelight is a singular luminosity;
quiet by nature—redemptive, reflective respite.

Centipede

Tonight coming up from the basement I notice
a two-inch centipede in the middle of the kitchen floor.

As I approach, it scurries.
I ask if it wants to go out as it heads toward the door.

I turn the knob, open the door,
and it hurries into the safety of darkness.

CHRISTINA

As the waitress we just met,
your timing is impeccable,
your observations astute,
suggestions perceptive,
your humor sublime,
your shoes so sensible;
we had a good time.

You are so capable
I would not be surprised
to also find out:
you drive a bus,
conduct the symphony,
are a magician,
mathematician,
drive a bulldozer Thursdays
for your uncle Zeb, are
three hours shy of an MBA,
study the likes of Bruno,
Spinoza, Descartes, Joyce.

Perhaps you can identify
all manner of bird, then
sing like them too
once they've been heard—
or charm flamingos,
play castanets,
all equally well
is one of my bets.

Direct observation informs
the nature of things,
we are lucky to notice
the joy that this brings;
if our vision is clear,
our intent honest,
our bias known.

Perhaps you dance ballet.

CIRCUMFERENCE

My awkward tongue
torques to articulate
such a dissimilar language.

FLAP NADDO JAMACH
PERSLIP GACHIO DUPH

I speak around my lack of knowledge,
slowly express the circumference of meaning;
they gesture and laugh good-naturedly.

KARCHU SOLZ DUNDUN

We eat leaves, drink bark tea.
I smile, try to imitate
their serious expressions.

Learning to eat every third day
and fast the rest, to push aside algae
before drinking from the stream,
where to find the psrazrgot root—

I live three months with my hosts,
learn many things,
stop thinking in English.

Come Home When You Can

Things my mother said:

Be kind to strangers; we are all going somewhere.

Don't use so much peanut butter—
that jar has to last us all week.

Tell the truth—seems simple enough;
don't hide your mistakes by making up stuff.

Come home when you can, she said,
Your father and I are here on the farm
waiting your safe return.

I return many times:

In sickness, in health, with girlfriends, without,
with joyous exuberance, burns, with injuries and doubt,
from hitchhiking New England in winter or fall
or across the country, I return from them all.

Once with a girlfriend with whom I was living,
we came to celebrate with family Thanksgiving;
the sleeping arrangement raised their alarm,
so to sleep together, we went to the barn.

I think about these things as the coroner
and funeral guys lift her unceremoniously
onto death's gurney, then wheel her
through the house and out the door.

COWBELLS

"The cowbells follow one another."
—*James Wright*

She settles down to write,
relaxing on the couch,
putting up her feet
so her ankles hang over the armrest.
Her writing becomes slower and slower,
eyelids descending closer and closer.
The notebook slips aside,
the pen tumbles to the floor.
She is asleep, we agree
when she starts to snore.

Her dream cows dot the hillside
almost too distant to be seen.
Among them one begins the turn,
then several, then more.
The barnward meander thus begun,
soon all follow—one, then one, then one.

We too hear the bells, find the path
and join the gather into the barn.
Each quietly writing though we shuffle
impatient feet, our papers begin to stir—
soon gradual discontent, vague in urge.
In our common sense we look about,
know the time to read aloud has come.

CHANCE, RHYTHM, RHYME

As she joins our pastoral scene,
to criticize does not occur.
She is the one who got a nap:
We all wish we were her.

DEAR TENDERNESS

Dear Tenderness,
the error how cute
and done so lovely,
you call me William
whenever we meet

I so willing
to be your William
do not correct,
let long years lapse,
perhaps forever.

How I love and adore you!
Always and ever,
Your William

HAIKUS

I
As we write haiku
the count is not obvious
quite apparently not.

II
Car is my safe place
so often there do my tears
freely tumble down.

III
Brittle ceramic
petals tumble down the wall
will you catch a few?

IV
Illuminated
gallery wall's blank canvas
waits for the artist.

V
Though he hurries on,
a rush in all he does now,
his shadow wanders.

VI
Keep poetry grounded,
let the thingness drive the work
of philosophy.

GATHERS

Contrarious octogenarians
grouped as young writers,
put on the bus,
start out strangers,
arrive as us.

DEAR LYNNE

Dear Lynne,

Thank you for your thoughtful response to the
book. Our dimensional reality is very interesting, the
push and pull of conscious awareness, the colors of
mind. Your timely visit to our street stopped (as it
were) in front of our house, and I as it happens,
noticed. It is as if all of nature had conspired with
geography, space, time, to permit our brief conversa-
tion. How good of you both to be willing to extend the
hand of friendship, kindness, through that window.

That you have found something in The Horse
Knows to like, and are willing to pay the poet, is
reassuring, though the check was not my primary
intent, but rather how we might as fellow creatures on
this water droplet we call Earth share and delight in
each other's unique and wondrous being.

Sincerely,
Steven

DO WE

Do we not shine,
do the stars not shine,
though the clouds obscure,
though we sleep through the night?

Do stars not shine,
though the sun's so bright
they're obscured in daylight—
do we not shine?

Though our conditions vary,
though we tire and grow weary,
if our source is divine
do we not shine?

DESERT SUNSET

Hot stone cliffs
reflect the heat of day
in spectral reds of sunset.

Evening creatures stir,
each movement calculated
toward survival.

He also begins, rolls out
from the crevasse of sleep,
stretches a yawn into wakefulness.

Establishing, in mind, direction,
prepared for the journey of night,
he tests his wings, then leaps.

Soaring west toward fading light,
the slash of lightning promises rain:
It is there he will hunt.

FALCON

"The falcon cannot hear the falconer."
—*Yeats*

The falcon has broken the bond,
no longer hears the falconer;
flights now her choosing,
no longer tethered to his will,
she sleeps free in nature,
lets hunger define the kill.

Writer, trouble the politics,
wander out the maze,
ponder past the obvious,
turn a truthful phrase.

GIFT

Not so green as envy, not so cold as ice,
sometimes it is useful, often something nice.

I
Today the gift is joy.
I awoke near sunrise troubled by a dream
of want and necessity, struggled at work
among competing imperatives,
seeking a path of honest recognition
to find a better idea.

Where is the joy? Follow the path.
Now the work is the same,
but the result is different,
more satisfying, more lovely, more grand.

II
Where is the gift of self?
How shall it be presented,
shown, made public?
Shall it be unwrapped,
tumbled from a box
taken down from the high place
to be used only on holy days?

Perhaps kept scrupulously hidden,
like a polished precious stone,
shown only to friends?

If we open up, let it pour forth
without measure: Joy will resound,
rebound, reply in harmonic voice.

III
A little stone, and rough,
without polish,
hardly of consequence,
put perhaps in the drawer
of small forgotten things,
yet there in patience waiting,
loving, hopeful, ready
for you to hold once more.

GOES

He goes someplace mental;
how he gets there is incidental—
he hardly minds a bit
in social shoes not meant to fit
since the pain is incremental.

HOPE

What a pester is hope—
so sure that life will continue unabated,
vigorous but unframed,
substantial as the swallow's nest
tucked in above the farmhouse door,
the birds returning year after year.

How vague is hope—
lean and slender,
a slip of light slanting through tall trees
to fall unbidden, a tender embrace
upon the sapling.

What a wonder is hope—
that, despite my distractedness,
art and form reside within,
await my return to conscious effort
at expression.

What a shear is hope—
ready to cut, to sever from my past
the confounding doubts of self-worth
and, in compassion, walk with me
around the corner into the sun.

How joyous is hope—
that even with the drama,
you still believe in me.

HOW HE WAS RAISED

He was raised by she wolves, taught manners,
to be aware, tough, and uncomplaining,
genuine, for they detect any fraud or conceit.

The sisterhood protected him when young,
but as an adult, he was always the other,
membership unavailable to him.

He learned discipline and distance,
self-sufficiency and survival,
when to be silent, when to run.

HUMMINGBIRD

Hummingbird in its flight through the front porch
pauses long enough to watch me through the window
as I type.
Feeling its presence, I look up and we engage duality.

Then it is gone. We both go back to work.

IN THE STILL

In the still of winter, ice melts,
silently slips through soil,
draws a vacuum,
aerating roots and microbes.

Quiet, but never still,
electrons traverse the mind
in the thrust of thought,
in loving embrace.

In the still dark,
the raptor's eyes hungrily perceive
the movement of prey;
talons flex patiently.

In the still soft morning
a mother is separated from her children
and disappeared into the bureaucracy
by Trumpian harm and conceit.

IRINA

Because you care enough
to look me in the eye
when you ask if I am well

And let the light
that is your smile
shine on me

I feel welcome
after a long day of travel
to be part of the family

Because you listen
when I speak
I have energy

If ever my son or daughter
do your job
I hope they emulate you

Because you are genuine,
pleasant, and kind
I send angels to fill your dreams

IT IS DONE

It is done, but not finished;
among the aspens whose leaves
quiver in the morning breeze,
the hole so stony is dug.

It is done, but not finished;
for fourteen years
the dog so joyous, so faithful,
falters and falls.

It is done, but not finished;
she walks her last few days
happily here at the farm,
her final appointment is made.

As you hold her head in your lap
the vet administers the shot;
her startled eyes look into mine
as she recognizes the end.

It is done, but not finished;
I turn away overcome by tears.
Later we lay her down
among the aspen trees.

JUST A POET

I am just a poet after all—
I notice, and emote of course,
and fall in love with you.
What did you expect
that I would do?

We could not predict,
nor had time to fret,
unaccompanied Bach
would become a duet.

LE JEU

I

The meme is French, the cards unpacked,
the rules declared, the chips are stacked.

The cards dealt clockwise, we begin the game;
instead, I stand my cards on edge to build a box.

When my turn comes to play, it interrupts my fun;
they've seen my cards; I say, "Pick one."

II

I prefer to complement rather than compete
let us work together on challenges we meet.

It is better than adrenaline
to have a group that lets all in.

And though none of us are tall
we can scale most any wall,

Split the neighbor's firewood
on the week they're gone,

Feed their dogs, do some good,
put flamingos on their lawn.

LIST

You must qualify, she said, to be on the list.
So I made application, sent tapes of supplication.

She texted me: Left undone
were references; I had none.

Dear strangers, acquaintances, friends:
Help me please to make amends,
even truth has some bends.

LONG LETTERS

Weigh the emotion,
value the intent
read each letter--
endure the void.

Our love is compassion,
our love is steel.

Grapple confusion,
endangered trust,
separate life lines
beyond shear capacity.

Our love is compassion,
our love is steel.

Spirit--
a trust,
a habit,
a view
too soon forgotten.

Our love is compassion,
our love is steel.

How shall I
be best,
be fair,
be kind,
without your love?

Our love is compassion,
our love is steel.

I am away with good intent,
working among strangers,
learning to do what is required,
as must be.

Our love is compassion,
our love is steel.

You are home
neither alone nor comforted
by the rigors of circumstance,
the routine of necessity.

Our love is compassion,
our love is steel.

The portion allotted--
balance, stability,
maddening desire,
the chill of sanity--

the empty without you is everywhere.
How I long for breath!

LUCK

Among the struggles, I find patience.
Among the tears, I find rest.
Among the disparate, I find connectedness.
Among the desolation, I find providence.
Among the bustle, I find calm.
Among the fears, I find confidence.
Among the years, I find playfulness.

LUCK OF THE AUTHOR

What? Luck?
How do you figure?
What shape is that?
A green bolder hat?

Being a goat in the machine
is hardly any advantage,
a poet has not even the prestige
of a. . .of a painter.

Rembrandt sued for libel,
but the court found not in his favor;
since he was a mere painter, it ruled
he had no status or reputation to protect.

A sanctity of calling,
inadvertent truth,
regrettably uncompensated,
a habit from my youth.

And yet: As luck would have it
writing breathes a life in me,
a calm expressive joy,
a combustible passion.

I have some interest, knowledge,
and capacity of speech,
the encouragement of friends,
and creative obligations to keep.

MOCKINGBIRD

The calm morning air outside welcomes;
in the yard a sunny rock.
Here I sit and with pocket knife
clean out the treads of my boots.

Next to me in a juniper bush
a mockingbird sings gloriously,
flies to a branch just over my head,
serenades briefly, then is silent.

I look up noticing it is very close,
staring at me intently,
cocking its head from side to side,
assessing, I suppose, my purpose.

I am cleaning my boots, I explain.
Each of us fascinated by the other.
Evidently it gets bored and flies off,
and I, grateful for conversation, smile.

NEW FIRE

The map pressed into the wet concrete
centuries ago is now archival knowledge.

Hyperlinks we share today keep us
constantly in the know; still, justice falters.

Power corrupts politics. Should we be surprised?
Has not it ever been thus? Were we born yesterday?

Let us then learn new ways to create community
that we might persevere in equitable causes.

NOT YOUR JOB

It's not your job, but still it's nice
you notice my trouble, give advice.

OUR SMALL TOWN

At the only traffic light in our small town,
I wait behind a logging truck
loaded with fourteen hemlock logs.
Behind me are three cars
and a tractor pulling a manure spreader.

The county office building, court house,
lawyer-type buildings, and a laundromat
are here because it is the county seat of power.

On the courthouse lawn stands a blackened
eight-by-ten-foot stone vault with an arched stone roof.
It once housed the Holland Land Company's
deeds and records. In 1836 its contents
were burned by protesting farmers.

An eight-point buck waits at the stop
for the traffic to clear,
then limps slowly across the road.

SCALE

From the tiny organism
to dragons,
from a grain of sand
to the largest mountain,
we owe our sense of rhyme
to the thinnest moment
and eons of time.

SHADOW

The shadow that crosses my path
is of a bird flying high overhead.

As we drink coffee on the porch
total strangers wave from their car.

SQUARES IN FOG

A wall of fog across the lake
has settled on the cold ice
in still morning air.

Sunlight illuminates the scene to my right,
while dense fog obscures everything to my left
as I look down on the scene from the roof.

Through the dense stationary cloud
I hear the bark of geese approaching
and though they are hidden from my view

I picture them flying just off each other's wing,
flapping in slow rhythmic cadence.
The shape of their calls seem square.

As they draw near, the squares grow in size,
increase in color and intensity—
variant, vibrant hues of yellow and green.

Suddenly right before me, they break free of the fog,
glide effortlessly toward a patch of open water,
and I see them as geese once more.

STAND IN THE HEART

Stand in the heart,
look out the window—
from this stance
see the path of justice;
follow it.
You will find friends.

As best of friends
we stand in the heart.
Though our participles
may not always agree,
though infinitives diverge,
still, with each other
we promote honest expression,
expect the best,
amplify the divine.

Someday best friends,
we work silently every day together
with hardly ever any conversation.
We have become,
we might be, friends.

We show up
whatever the weather;
we don't complain,
we do our work, go home.

Some days at lunch

we sit next to each other,
notice our commonality,
though lives are disparate.

STANDING

Beyond my outstretched arm
a thumb thrusts upward

Beyond the thumb
a string, arching white line

Beyond the line
a kite jostles

Beyond the kite
a cloud pauses

Beyond the cloud
a blue satin

beyond the blue
a moon.

STEVE'S REPLY

The wind is cold,
blowing thoughts of snow.

The night is dark,
the hour is late and though

The tide is out,
it will return, I know.

My harbor heart rejoicing swells
and, finally, lets go.

The promise is the future.
The blessing is today.

We feel the promise turning spring,
marvel in the chapel of love,
the cathedrals of nature,
the immediacy of time.

We hope for a better tomorrow
but live today,
work for the respect of friends,
endeavor, trust.

STONE WALLS

The leaves have not yet burst forth.
I can see the stone walls among the trees—
walls that crisscross, undulate,
that span three centuries
since settlers pushed the natives out,

incidental walls created to satisfy
the needs of the plow,
stones carried to perimeter edges
to create fields where once
boreal forests stood,

walls built by men and women,
daughters and sons, stone by stone
hefted and labored onto cart or sled
in winter, in rain, in fall,

those trees clear-cut for lumber
or burnt to ash, then mixed with lye,
making the soap that shipped
on vessels returning to England.

One estimate for these walls
indicates the accumulated length
might exceed 250,000 miles,
ten times around the earth.

SYRUP

Before the thaw,
taps are set,
buckets hung.

The warmth of March,
the chill at night,
cycle the sweet flow.

Amish neighbors collect,
pour into large casks
on horse-drawn sleds.

Stacks of firewood
laid up in late fall
await the boil.

THE END AND LAST

From the modest perch of Grandpa's knees,
I could see the end of trees,
the last survivors they cut down.
It was not malice, just disregard
that had them taken from the yard
by men who came from town.

THE GIFTS OF YOU

You arrive bearing great gifts;
the gift of your perception,
the joy of your smile,
the warmth of generosity
you bring to the room,
your welcome embrace
of the differences
with strangers in our midst,
the presence of your knowledge,
transformative, informed.

The perceptive inquiry
you bring to every quest
is one of your qualities
that I like the best.
So important is the effort
you give to every line,
more important than the rhyme.
Most valuable of all
is the gift of your time.

One gift that you gave me
is that someday I might,
at least learn to read,
so one day I write.

THE SUN

The sun gets out her umbrella.
I hold it over her as we walk in rain.

THE WORD

"The word is the taste."
—*Rosario Castellanos*

The word is the taste, be it pleasant or foul—
expressed with the tongue as consonant, vowel.

Rain is just rain, a curse or a blessing—
defined in our mind, often by guessing.

THEN THE STARS

Houses here are side by side,
though it's the place where I reside.
From our house atop the hill
we hear each siren blare
and watch the traffic crawl below
and the storms that bring snow.

As I type, across my screen
reflected images of clouds
in the sun's fading light,
then late at night, the stars.

THEN THE TEARS

Then the tears came,
because he paid attention,
because it was their turn,
their time of the month,
a Tuesday.

Because he no longer distressed about them
they were now friends enough to embrace.
Sometimes he could see them afar off,
estimate how long their trek would take,
if their stay would be brief or extended,
would they bring amusement or incapacity.

Let the storm surge, he thought,
as wave after wave washed over him.
He has learned to relax,
let them buffet and turn him
without inducing panic.

THEY DO NOT SEE HER

She was the first woman
to run for the school board.
The men asked amused,
"How does she expect to get elected
without a business background?"

They underestimated Mom,
her quiet efficiency, passion for education,
belief in creative capacity,
and her experience doing a man's job
at the steel mill during the war.

The family is not surprised she won,
but the businessmen are.
Many women say, It is about time!
The celebration is proper,
sheet cake served.
Those men do not attend.

For the next six years
she asks awkward, difficult questions.
"Is the teacher fired just because he's gay?"
"Why are we punishing students for protesting
injustice and war?"
"Isn't it our job to educate all our students?"

As her term expires,
she does not seek another, saying,
"It is someone else's turn."

TODAY

Today you don't see me
with my eyes swollen shut
by a bite, or a sting,
or some other thing.

You will not know
that my energy is low
that I am sad
and politics are bad.

This poem in a fashion
has grain like our passion—
shows our history, our stress,
complicated awkwardness.

TRIP

"Dad I have a week," he says, "to spend with you.
Just tell me what you want to do.
Anywhere in the world to go
you get to choose. Let me know."

Argentina, Alaska, Spain
immediately were in my brain,
adventures swirling in my head,
but I said this instead:

"Son, help me do a puppet show.
It's in St. Paul. D'you want to go?
The festival is in July."
"Are you sure?" was his reply.

At the National Puppetry Fest
among the many we weren't the best,
yet still we were pretty good,
got the applause I hoped we would.

TWO MEN IN SNOW

Father and son
both grown men
backs to the wind
squatting in snow
eat their lunches
on the hill top
in February howl.

Behind them are
the grapevines trimmed,
the frigid morning
accomplished.

UNWRAP THE GIFT

Unwrap the gift of obstacles,
hold it forth in light.

Try to crack it with the teeth,
disengage it from the craw.

Walk around it, see the back,
deduce the reason that it troubles so,

what makes up its foundation,
validates concern.

Deconstruct the history,
why its presence ruffles.

Let new questions redefine,
pull its plug of power.

UTILITY WORK

The crew is here early doing utility work;
cutting out the cancer, cauterizing,
stitching, prepping for resurfacing.

I look in the mirror
and adjust my attitude for the day.
I look for the list of questions,

rework my assumptions,
look like brown crispy crust,
redefine the value for time.

VISION OF TIME

Growth-based perception,
peripheral knowledge,
unfocused knowing:

What can we also learn
that is peripheral?
Mist on the face
ungrasped by hands,

how we grow
complex and unattended,
not by will or wanting
but by finding
what's already blooming,

witnessing our lives,
what is revealed in our expectations
as we express the process of being.

What delight in the ambiguity!
What is the unknowable probability
of our existence?

We write our part each day;
the doing is our witness, our telling,
spontaneous expression.

WEBS

Webs in the window—
the silver strands
catch and pronounce
angular morning light.

WEIGHT OF ACCUMULATION

Though the weight of the past is strong,
let it fill the heart with joy, with song.
As we know the springtime shower
will help the bud become a flower
so we too must let go
if we expect to grow.

The past we try to keep as things
will hinder us in use of wings.
By letting go, we show our trust;
if we're to fly, we must, and so
our song becomes more sweet,
and we more free to leave our feet.

We Stay Up All Night

We stay up all night
making maps of topography,
maps of contour,
with shape, depth, elevation.

We stay up all night
while the women drive Alex home
because his grandmother died
and he consoled himself with alcohol.
We men, left unattended,
write silently—fictitious, graphic,
humorous prose and poetry.

We stay up all night waiting for friends
to arrive on the 3:00 a.m. bus,
which is, by the way, now two hours late,
the result, we speculate,
of yet another event in the desert.

We stay up all night
walking the neighborhood
with flashlights,
calling quietly for Quincy,
my daughter's cat.

We stay up all night
watching the ham-sized egg hatch.
My dad kept it warm for eight weeks
behind the fridge. He said the heat

given off by the condenser coils
was just the right temperature.
Claiming he found it,
he nested it in some old towels.
He checks it every evening. But we
suspect he is hatching it for a friend
whose wife would have none of it.

We stay up all night pre-celebrating graduation
and find the 11:00 a.m. ceremonies awkward.
Even lining up alphabetically is a challenge.
Sleepily we shuffle and yawn as we process in,
then slouch into our seats. During the presentation,
several classmates exit to use the bathrooms.
Everyone feels better when they return.

WHAT LUCK FOR US

As luck would have it,
I find I have lost the list of aggravations
I was going to share with you.

I also seem to have lost my lists of
medical concerns, hostilities,
and grumbling ingratitude.

As luck would have it,
just before you arrived
I found my sense of humor—

it was buried under
the paperwork on my desk.
And I found time to bake!

Yet When You

You mock, chortle,
amused by my effort
to clean the basement,

and yet, when you visit,
if I have a chance to impress,
it may be there.

YOU ATTRACT ME

"In the mathematical field of differential geometry, a
metric tensor is a type of function which takes as input a
pair of tangent vectors v and w at a point of a surface (or
higher dimensional differentiable manifold) and produces
a real number scalar $g(v, w)$ in a way that generalizes many
of the familiar properties of the dot product of vectors in
Euclidean space. In the same way as a dot product, metric
tensors are used to define the length of and angle be-
tween tangent vectors. Through integration, the metric
tensor allows one to define and compute the length of
curves on the manifold."

—*Wikipedia*

You attract me—your lines of force pull on me.
I am drawn into your gravitational well.
The very idea of you awakes me like morning sun.

Interest and permission will not stay unconscious.
My mind is unresolved, ambiguities unbalance;
on this sphere, lines have no parallel.

YOU MIGHT THINK

You might think I never get tired,
or angry, or glum—
like tonight, I turn on my brain,
and all I hear is . . . hum.

YOUR BOAT

"The lamp swings in an arc."
—*David Bell*

I
Internal shadows dance back and forth;
arise, descend as harmonic horizon
energy waves ebb and flow—
how will the story end?

II
The wide arc of sentiment—
pondered potentials, loss,
resounds with sonar echo
in winter river harbors

the arc of each footfall overhead
on the deck in measured stride,
measured in mind, anticipated:
one, two, three, and a half.

III
The stretch of fingers slashes
the keyboard—navigational notes,
draw out each line of meter depth,
the pound per foot of his Saturna

the bearing lift of every swell,
heave and lean of every breeze,
as temperatures of evening fall
the edges begin to freeze.

2018

ASSEMBLAGE

Writers group:
eyes slantered, shut,
minds intent, restful,
focused, azure, sublime

fingers flashing keystrokes
pencil eraser drifting nub,
pen scrawls heavy edits
another text on the phone.

Windows sunshine rectangles,
the wind outside is chill,
each writer here in earnest,
each expressing still.

BE PATIENT, DEATH

Be patient, death,
as I walk each step,
I am in no hurry.

BE SKEPTICAL

I
His creative self was stalled by politics that appalled.
Daily it became more clear he was justified to fear.

II
Why is it, do you suppose, that political fund-raising
campaigns and organizations send me requests to sup-
port their war chests. Do they not understand what the
word "war" means? Do they know more civilians are
killed in war than combatants? Have they never lost a
loved one to a bullet, a bomb dropped for that very pur-
pose? Have they never carried a bleeding child while they
look for water, for safety?

Do they not see what is happening in Syria, Sudan,
Afghanistan, and the many other war-torn countries in
the world. Why would the they use the vile, repulsive
word war to solicit funds from us to use in the election
of public servants? I for one, refuse to give any money
for a war campaign.

III
Be skeptical. Corporations are not your friend.
They are here to eat you, and your children.

IV
There is a saying in sports, "You are exactly
what your record says you are"—Bill Parcells.
What does our record say about our country?
A nation of free thinkers? Do we delude ourselves?

With a history of slavery and genocide, what are we?
Our governmental policies more often
overthrow democracies to empower dictators
than promote decency, fair play, and good will;
that disenfranchises most of the population
and is economically, politically, racially unjust.

V

What are we willing to do that will create change?
"Who's streets? Our streets!" is chanted
during a counter march in Boston.

These streets do not belong to the mayor
or other authority;
these streets belong to the people.

We are not guests of the government
when we march; we do not need
their permission to be here!

BIRD

The bird dies hitting the window,
then falls to the roof below.

A workman notices it there,
hoping it will fly, tosses it in the air.

It does not flutter; he watches it fall
without much cheer into the garden.

The gardener finds it beside the yellow mum,
tenderly sets it on the porch rail.

The morning sun casts its long shadow
across the temple wall.

Each day the boy, on his way to school,
touches it with blessing.

One night a cat, not yet full grown,
carries it away.

The boy observing the empty space,
knows that it has flown.

CONFERENCE OF BIRDS

These uncommon birds
arrive from many directions,
in buffeted flight descend at dusk.
They walk in silent communion
a snowy path laboring uphill;
footprints, temporary statements of intent,
purposeful in turn, accumulate.
One, two, several, a dozen,
each unique and wonderful,
patterning three-toed feet.

DEAR FRIEND

Dear Friend,

As usual I am at a loss for words,
how to counsel, advise, console you.
The death of a loved one, sudden or elongated,
harsh or merciful, unfair or well earned,
whether by attack of violence
or accomplished in great calm,
is a passage for them and for us.

What was seems to be no more.
Our love, joy, angst, our agitation with them,
seem perhaps in retrospect so temporary.
The sense of loss, of anger, sadness, are the result
of loving bonds woven in earnest endeavor
over long years of trust,
sudden capacities for honesty,
engendered emotions,
personal challenges, insights.

The relative nature of reality,
attended as it must be by our point of view,
some may burn in precise focus,
others in the most causal moments,
yet always we image permanence.

The abrupt nature of death startles us
by temporariness.

Love,
peace,
holding,

Steven

DEAREST SIR AND MADAM

Dearest Sir and Madam,
And we for our part,
wanting to linger 'til the evening's end
did perhaps stretch your patience, true.

If therein you find some fault,
forgive the hour that we depart
from honest reverie in your gracious love,
that we may in future make a mend.

DIAMETER

I
Girth,
seminal width,
reliable choices,
function of math+2R.

Relevant choices,
imply round:
the Latin term
does not predate the wheel.

II
Dia-meter—
equipped to measure,
aimed to ascertain,
display knowledge.

III
And you, standing unafraid,
ready and fierce,
calm and patient,
write metaphorically.

IV
Lull asleep the giant matters,
walk silent, light footsteps let fall,
breathe deep among the shadows,
and dream lovely most of all.

FORECAST

It was predictable,
but not part of the forecast.
That part was delayed
and arrived after the fact.

For a fisherman, each cast's
a hope for a better future,
yet his catch mostly, is the past,
a tangle of filaments.

We agree the unknown
is perplexing to forecast,
yet we proceed to chance, with joy,
with regard, in peace.

Past experience helps us
jump the brook, avoid the wet,
lay down our arms,
disencumber the present,
agree to terms,
promote the possible,
risk some comfort,
embolden trust.

GUEST

A guest for the day, you permit my presence
in mutual interest and thus share space time.

The awkward shuffle of feet and packages
while in line at the post office,

the group consciousness and chill
waiting for the bus of February,

at the big food market deli bustle,
numbers, impatience, shouting,

Pooch and panting at the dog park
waiting for the gate that only swings out.

CHANCE, RHYTHM, RHYME

I AM WILLING

I am glad you find something to like unfolding.

Your email gets to the core and lets me cry,
honestly seeing what's in the mirror.

For me to write is like breath and why,
easy or labored, I'm willing to try.

I WRITE

I write up in the attic.
It has a small window at each end.
Most of the roof is too low
to allow me to stand.
In the east window sit flower pots;
not all of the plants are alive.

As I type this I am wearing
a hat and jacket
and though I have
a small space heater
eighteen inches from my knees,
hardly is it effective.

To warm my fingers, I hold
a mug of honey lemon tea,
a winter staple
of Korean neighbors.
A solitary fruit fly
is drawn by the aroma.
I notice but do it no harm.

This space is not
the main function of this house.
While certainly advantageous,
it is not convenient;
useful, but it requires
the commitment to climb narrow stairs
and, under dim light,
purposefully accomplish.

IS THAT YOUR HAND?

I
Is that your hand
in the cookie jar?

Is that your hand
under the table?

Is that your hand
in my pocket?

Is that your hand
without consent?

Is that your hand
on his throat?

Is that your hand
over my mouth?

II
Is that your hand
raised in protest?

Is that your hand
seeking justice?

Is that your hand
volunteering?

Is that your hand

asking questions?

Is that your hand
building community?

Is that your hand
helping others?

IT'S NO SMALL COMFORT

Gravity still draws the knife
that falls as guillotine
in unfortunate necessity
to void the rule of king.

JUAN

Juan has gone outside,
though the air so chilly
the sun does not warm.
Across the river horizontal views
draw out what he holds inside.

On his artist pad,
across the unlined paper
he draws fresh ink borders,
in the architecture of words
shadows of birds, shadows of will.

Pen to mouth, pen to paper,
hand steady as a carpenter,
he grips the tool of penmanship,
writes with conviction,
with passion nails each sound.

Squirrels leap from tree to roof
above his wicker seat
that seems too low for serious business,
the table too, absurdly so,
both designed for sloth of summer.

Returning to join companions
he reads aloud, unique and wonderful long lines
of poetry that challenge the breath.
His strong percussive voice, cadence and confidence,
persuade us in feet, in meter, in jest.

What a joy, a pleasure to watch you work.
In the sharing, our lives expand, we learn much.

KISS

Your smile, so disarming, brightens the room—
how useful this holiday season.

Although your kiss has no name,
it sizzles with quandary, like an Argentinian
proverb.

More fascinating, it evolves over time
from edgy pluralism to soft, lingering caress.

MICHAEL

What love we send,
peace we send,
in this time of tears.

Express the sense of loss
as only you must know,
let go the spirit souls.

Embrace the family, friends;
share what you can, and release
to the comfort of angels.

MOVEMENT

Tonight she will sit principal.
As audience, I settle in the second row
long before she walks on stage.

The crowd talks loudly
as the orchestra warms up.
She laughs with a colleague.

A suited stagehand brings out the score
placing it on the conductor podium
matter-of-factly in the cacophony.

As she plays the cello,
her white skirt edged in lace
draws taut across her knees.

During the horn concerto,
a woman next to me unravels her knitting;
the variant lavender strand simulates her outfit.

I notice the horn player's tie
matches the brass of his instrument.
A dying moth flutters at his feet during the solo.

Between movements
the cellist wipes rosin from strings;
on cue she strums the cello like a guitar.

Not Yet Dark

Under trees
in the green spectrum
we gather.
It is not yet dark

Pottery, fire,
science, steam
contained in space,
water, pressure, force.

Whistles, bells—
rotors, cams, gears,
pistons, wheels, clocks;
from the forge, iron rails.

Finest china tea sets,
industrial mills and death,
the arc of arrows,
the frightful reach of lance.

It is not yet dark,
but darkness is coming.

War victims make no rhymes,
migrant camps fester despair;
the stock market doesn't care
how the darkness comes.

Not yet dark
fading light
getting dark
twilight
light enough
nearly dark
darker
quite dark
dark.

PERHAPS/WINDOW

All winter the window has waited
to be unstuck, to be open—
the air so chill that was avoided—
permitted into the house at last!

Spring, full of esters, full of promise,
daffodils shouldering through snow,
bridal wreath in tender leaf,
so small, so ready, bees notice.

Before the sun is rising,
before the noise of man,
before regrets are spoken,
before the song of birds,
the petal flock is buzzing,
the juniper berry taste,
awake I sing, imagine
what has now begun.

RATTLE IN THE WIND

The old oak at the precipice,
the edge of gravity,
the edge of usefulness,
for two centuries
survives deformity.

Other trees were long ago
harvested for lumber
or burnt to ash in stoves,
in furnaces shaping steel,
making soap for Europe.

Twisted, awkward branches
arc low, stretch wide.
Long crotches slope to heaven
in unique dissymmetry
that reminds me:

Rattle in the wind,
reach, blossom,
tremble,
resolve,
be.

RESIST

Resist the torrent of words that disrespects speech,
stand for honesty, earnest endeavor.

Resist the ilk of harm that corruption breeds,
grow in grace, abide no slander.

Resist the tyrant rant, resolve to be unafraid,
attach with value the barnacles of persistence.

Resist, and with friends willing to stand in union,
grow in common good, endorse emancipation.

Align the prop with forces that allow all to prosper,
be strong when tempers flare, be calm.

Among those who do not show, be disappointed
but be not dismayed. They are not you.

Walk the path you know as best. Be fair in council.
If you tire, take a rest, let go, 'til the 'morrow.

Self-Portrait

I
Because my self-portrait with the muskrat
had gone so well, I thought to find a seal.

Flying from the Midwest to California
I consider how much fun this will be.

Oh, to bask among the seals, bark our stories, nap.
In my wetsuit out on the craggy rocks, I wait alone.

II
A drawing
A line
A result

Drawing imaginary
lines of poetry
results in fiction

Drawing from the past
nonlinear thoughts
resolve happenstance

Drawing nigh appreciation,
a long line of compliments—
will you receive mine?

III
Walk the creek to find me

walk barefoot in grass
sing the song of warbler, wren
evolve the present, let it pass.

Counterbalance force with patience,
help the sunshine light dark places,
speak not with adder tongue,
be tender, kind, to unknown faces.

Grow in peace with inspiration.
Let go the myth of Adam's Apple.
From dispirit venture forth,
find in thyself the chapel.

SHE LIVES IN LAWRENCE, KANSAS

She lives in Lawrence, Kansas.
The threshold of her yurt with door rolled up,
under which I enter, welcomes me as friend.

The pen I use to write this poem
is brand new, thus undisciplined,
has yet to write numbers, knows no math,
expresses disregard for structure,
composes text that has no path.

Because I'm kind, well mannered,
she meets me at the restaurant
but will not tell me secrets
unless I am a confidant.

Some days it is enough not to cry,
enough to begin again, to try.

SUPPOSE-ITRY

Hypothetically, might it be poetry?
How it could be more than would be,

Imagine dynamic futures, permit the possible,
embrace unknowns, engage the energy.

SWEET SONG

The distraught young rose finch
chirps sporadically.
Somehow it has traversed
the rotating door into the hotel lobby.

Beyond the glass
its parents respond in desperation.
Their emotive cries
call to me.

Around the frightened bird,
I cautiously wrap my jacket.
Once outside, I kneel
beside a shrub and release it.

Immediately both parents land near,
chirping excitedly.
Their reunion is joyous.
What a sweet song is life.

THE GATE

The gate, unlocked, unbroken;
fears impede what's unspoken;
reach out your hand, and open.

THINGS HAPPEN

Sometimes things happen.
I always assumed I would
be there and able:
to put out the toaster fire,
to catch you,
to know the story,
to help you heal,
to be part of us.

THIS PAINTING

On a fall Sunday afternoon when I was around fourteen, my folks, seeing I was bored and despondent, said, "We are taking you to the Albright Knox Art Gallery."

"But, Mom—"

"Son, we are not to argue. Let's go."

After an hour's drive we arrived. The entry fee was an extravagant expense for my folks. They did not complain. I was intrigued, smitten with the color and largeness of the modern paintings hanging on the grand white walls. We walked and gazed, discussed and wondered, gestured and pointed. It was then that I knew I was to be an artist.

Leaving the building, we passed by the gift shop. Please, please, I implored, can we buy some paints? In the end, they said yes. We bought a half dozen small tubes of oil paints and a tablet of paper.

After chatting most the way home, we arrived at my grandparents' house for the usual Sunday dinner. I immediately took the paints out of their box but realized we had not bought a brush. I found a plastic fork and used that to move the paint around. I was called to the dinner table several times but refused until the painting was done.

This painting of a tornado is the result. The little red barn being overwhelmed by the debris field is, I suppose, how I felt at the time. After fifty years, being an artist is still what I love most doing. What a joyous and interesting life! Thanks, Mom and Dad!

THREE QUESTIONS, THREE ANSWERS

I
Why and what causes you
to hesitate, to stammer,
to fumble thoughts
so close to expressing?

I, I, I, Be-because-cause
m-m-my m-m-mind
is a-a-large and
c-cavernous space.

It is not m-made-up or tidy.
It is stirred by deep emotion,
churned by tectonic forces,
engaged elsewhere.

II
Why now?

Because now is the right time,
this moment, enduring present,
endeavoring synaptic relevance,
embracing spatial consensus.

III
Why repeat what you know already?

I repeat, I repeat,
because it is mantra, the mantra,

is cloth and circumstance,
is depth and breathing.

The grocery store is like a theater, like therapy;
it is full of drama in the fish department,
catharsis in canned goods, the angst of freezer burn,
the joy and jostle of the checkout line.

UNTWINE II

This space was reserved for "Untwine."
It is removed at the author's request.

Here is what he said:

"Untwine": Please remove this poem.
Though I like the poem
and think it does the work I ask of it,
it feels too raw and truthful.

The edges of this event still hurt
when I hear them in my mind;
to speak them out loud
seems unbearable.

WE ARE NOT ONLY HUMAN

Beyond what we perceive,
we are not only human.

Beyond the past, before the rain,
beyond nostalgic memories,
chance encounter,
happenstance.

The writers like bricklayers,
once the prompt lines are placed,
work with trawls and mortar;
shink, shink, slath, dab, splat, brick.
Brick, brick, shink, shink, dab, slath, splat.

Sweets brought from India
sustain, inform, and guide
as we type and scrawl in hurried motion,
determined efforts, destined in time.

We celebrate the boatman's return;
like little flags, we wave and flap.

YOU

The butterfly flaps her wings;
you, like the space between,
float in air,
abrupt, subtle, sudden,
relaxing, gliding in light.

2019

ARE YOU ABLE

Are you able
in the heat of Da Nang
to be still as the Yellow Buddha,
as the Marble Mountain,
as long rays of early sun
silhouette trees so near the water?

Are you able
in the dark of winter
to follow the young man's gait,
allow him the lead of inspiration,
follow the point of his finger
when he says, "There!"

Are you able
to chance and abide the embrace
of community with strangers,
purpose the breath with mindfulness,
willingly disarm judgement?

Are you able
to calm nervous humor
let moments appreciate, gather,
unregulate expectations enough,
to, like a cat, just be?

AS SHE WALKS

As she walks along
what was lost is found

The corners of her mind
become unhinged, unbound

As she walks along
alarms begin to sound

Will her life too soon end
before it turns around?

BEES

I
The bees in lavender,
the bees in mint.

Late summer bees still pause in flight
to wander the flower stem.
We also seek to find the sweet.

Where can the scent of nature
lurk among the concrete towers,
theft for profit, wealth, and power?

II
The bees in lavender,
the bees in mint.

The figures of eighty-two children,
cast in bronze, stand stoically in the rain
on the memorial Lidice lawn.

It is the site where the Nazis
put children on trains
bound for death in ovens.

III
The bees in lavender,
the bees in mint.

Black babies and toddlers

were stolen and used
as alligator bait in Florida.

The Sacred Text does not save them,
or prevent us
putting immigrant children in cages.

    IV
The bees in lavender,
the bees in mint.

The bees still gather,
at the edge of the knife,
at the edge of night.

BROKEN WINGS

I
I find the broken wing;
I say, "Let me press you."
I prep the iron, setting it to silk.
The iron glides across the wrinkles.
It looks better but will not fly.

II
I find a broken wing in the cemetery;
I wonder which angel lost it.
Are they flying in a circle, looking for it?
If it loses a wing, does a new one grow in its place?
This one is made of marble.
Whom should I call to say it has been found?

III
I find a wing.
There is writing on it
in a language I do not speak,
I do not understand.

IV
I find a wing—is it yours?
I ask eleven people at the park.
Only one responds at all;
he is seven.

V
Are you the one who fixes
furniture and things?

Among the remedies you know,
do you know the one for wings?

VI
One of my wings feels broken;
I can see in the mirror it's hanging askew.
Can you help? Do you have
the proper type of glue?

BUREAUCRACY

I

First they sort, with a fist,
who is tall, who is short
report it all, make a list

Weight, class, harmonic
so deadly and moronic
contagious and bubonic

Pull from the upper shelf
behind a box of memes
the jar of broken dreams.

II

Look in the Hall of Records,
find the cabinet marked: Lost

It is in the corner closet
under the shelf of spools

Open the bottom drawer
pull out the folder most worn

Among the letters from lovers,
you'll find there some from me.

CHANCE, RHYTHM, RHYME

"The dogs bark, but the caravan moves on."
—Arab proverb

The window has no screen,
and doors are left askew;
sometimes I feel amiss.
I wonder if you do.

Son and daughter, find balance.
Once done, set your feet.
Blithely step into the light,
be genuine with those you meet.

The window has no screen;
the sunlight and the dew
spill in upon my open heart,
open because of you.

The window has no screen,
the door is left ajar,
the future might be full of choice,
but now is where we are.

With help from strangers, friends,
we find our way, in light or dark—
fear not what might be there,
although the dogs may bark.

So let us be up and doing;
like dreams, let us occur—
beyond what might be just enough,
jump in the pot, and stir.

COURAGE

More than being strong, we have courage,
if we're wrong, to make a mend and heal.

Mustering the will to disarm hurt,
courage lets the heart still feel.

Let courage, gumption, start each day,
the needs of doing, chance and choose.

Courage from the ground builds up,
especially if we wear no shoes.

Day Awakens

The day awakens slowly,
as is proper for awareness
to come about
toward events and action.

Toes still wet from wading
in hyper-consciousness,
wet in the shadows of light,
they test for comfort, for purpose,
to put aside blankets of doubt.

By noon, the day spins,
bickers, swims—
in the lush of brilliance,
exaltation.

Finally, the day leaps
into the deep of night,
into oblivion,
not in remorse or struggle,
but in sweet, exhausted surrender,
in the peace of letting go.

We observe it setting,
beyond the horizon,
beyond our control,
in the knowing
we too must let go.

Early Light

In the early light,
as the flycatchers
prepare their nest
for a second brood,

the barnyard cat
on the stone wall
patiently awaits
a young chipmunk.

Across the creek
a gray squirrel dashes
under shadows of
a flight of crows.

FOG

Water condensing heavy,
thick clouds landing,
wet hair drips down
our necks.

Happily we face the wind,
happily we chatter on,
salted nostrils of ocean air,
bare feet in sand.

FOR WHAT

I
What am I looking for,
what is the layer of dust concealing,
the sadness not revealing,
in my past—
what is the scar that so needs healing?

II
For what do I hope
that finds you so appealing,
that bends a prayer like kneeling,
the temper of annealing—
is it real, or just a feeling?

HOW CONCISE YOUR LOVE

How concise your love
with proper edging, borders.

No ambiguity, no stray hairs,
everything fixed and tidy.

The dermatologist says,
"You've got nothing."

We celebrate,
we dance.

HUMAN HEART/AI

From outside we see quite well
past reach of the corporate spell.
Beyond the paper design of tech
wait better ideas in retrospect
with no doubt that lingers—
precise, piston, robotic fingers.

Machines that poke, pry, and prod,
do the things once left to God.
We trust, repeat, big pharma views
that daily chloroform the news.
Without the need for caring sighs
they'll come tomorrow for our eyes.

LEVERS

Among the shapes and shadows
with levers of truth
we unearth our spiritual nature,
unfurl our angel wings.

I watched a man today who knew
what God intended him to do.

He showed, by his very being,
how to live a life of meaning.
He never spoke at a hurried pace
and wore contentment on his face.

LONGEST NIGHT/SHORTEST DAY

I
Soon the days will
stop getting shorter,
the light get brighter.

II
The darkness like a bundle,
a burden, a weight on the brow,
heavy in mind, thick as stubbornness,
will finally begin receding.

III
Like a slow drain
that shows no perceptional movement—
like the car I've left in neutral
in a parking lot with no discernible slope
that, as I leave the store,
I watch roll across the street,
through the other lot, bound a ditch,
and come to rest in un-mowed clover—
As I look about, no one seems to notice
or be concerned, so I casually walk over
and drive away.

IV
Time slips away like the night,
imperfectly drives off
like the back side of a second,
the silent space behind the tick,

the other weight on the fulcrum,
the transitional moment
in the arc of the pendulum,
a pause in breath.

V
Time is contemporary,
a contrivance,
an illusion.
It is light,
not the hard shell
we call reality.

MAKE A LIST

MATH	LEFTNESS
tape	Yearn
glue	lea
pasta	shadow
paste	soul

GRAVITY	GRIP
water	rough
down	plummet
tides	grasp
orbit	slip

GATHERS	ENTRUST
community	chance
flocks, feathers	balance
dancing fools	gift
annoyances	time

ASPIRE	GRAMMAR
points	spelt
energy	awkward
boundaries	diagram
hunger	splice

CHANGE	HOPE
necessity	attire
pinch	mirth
pressure	direction
pull	breath

NAPS

Naps are recommended
by doctors in magazines;
cats especially,
even dogs, take naps.

But for me? Not today,
I am in a funk.
Besides, it is already 5:00 p.m.—
who takes a nap this late in the day?

I am discouraged knowing
that the time I spend writing this poem
I could have taken—
a nice refreshing nap.

Though I have not yet done so,
because I am an optimist—
I think I might take one tomorrow,
or maybe, probably, the next day.

NO HAUNT

I find no haunt in nature,
even death—the hunt's sublime.
The only haunt I find is man.

Nature can be terrifying,
unforgiving,
yet
a glorious, raucous joy.

NO SPACE IS EMPTY

No space is empty.
Something lives there:
perhaps hope, opportunity, desire.

You think yourself a void,
a place where no winds blow,
unredeemable dark?

Ha! I see generous potential,
the sharp edge of flint
waiting to be struck.

You must trust the glow within;
even on the dark days,
your embers await the smallest breeze,

ever ready to ignite and fill
the heart and hearth with warmth,
and so dispel the fog of doubt.

OUT THERE

I feel you out there
perhaps two, three days distant,
a wave that will toss and turn
this little boat around.

I feel you out there
reliably unavoidable,
jostling and abrupt as a bus,
unsettling my emotions.

PAUSE

A space in time to un-hitch, for breath—
relax the need to swim against the tide.

Let go the wounding spring,
untwirl the fever pitch,

find a harmonic pace,
let worry flee the face.

PLEASE KNOW

Please, you must know:

I wish you well,
the hope of joy,
the work of love.

In peace the welcome
of newness, adventure,
that is each day.

With care and tenderness,
in all things
wonders abide.

Love,
peace,

Steven

Rake

The rain rake was too dull
to be of much use.

Sharpen your tools,
handle with care:
Don't suffer fools,
plan and prepare.

READ OUT LOUD

Read out loud
though it makes you cry.
Pick from the jar of words,
open the box, let out the wind,
untrouble the heart, release the sigh.

Read out loud this poem
with breath saved for this purpose,
saved from the holiday chatter,
collected in bits like oxygen,
exhaled as dew on the juniper.

Read out loud
in joy of hopefulness;
in the work of community
contribute anew with glee,
look not for recompense.

Read out loud—
declare the path of stars,
traverse the heavens,
see there the verb, the noun
in perfect present tense.

READY, DRESSED

At 10 a.m. I begin to cry
on the first day of Spring.
I sit on the floor.

The wind goes through this house
as if there were no walls,
and thoughts of you fly through me
unobstructed by time.

In occasional sun,
my thoughts, emotions,
are deflected, bleating—
long, slow waves
unbalance my soul.

Like the warmth of sunshine
on my hopeful skin,
you are a welcome relief
from the chill of winter.

Once more, I begin to find
my way, and bring my best:
Be ready, dressed,
knocking at your door.

SIMULTANIUM

Time is a pretty mess—
untidy, unruly, brittle,
a lingering, luscious tussle
of what is, what might, what's not.

Time is a pretty mess—
often too much, too little,
a healer of mind and muscle,
remembering hopes forgot.

Time is a pretty mess—
predictive, strategic, committed,
in the pull of distant stars,
like you, so terribly hot.

The truth is told in paradoxes;
dreams still weep in fancy boxes.

SKATEBOARDING

Have courage to try.
if you get hurt,
it's okay to cry.

Remember, life is not a race;
we each learn at our own pace.

Get up, dust off your duff;
get better ideas, be tough.

THE BLIND MAN AND THE MOON

The blind man fails to see the moon
or hear it passing overhead,
or phasing new,
or knows the slip of it waxing.

Yet the blind man knows
the pull of it, to balance
the shift in his stance,
whether it be up or set.

THE TEXT OF BIRDS

While I write, I turn off
the outdated flip phone,

the one that does not text,
the one my children almost never call,

the one on which the airline won't alert me
that my flight is delayed, my luggage found.

It is only a device for speaking;
it will not give directions or advice

or tell me if a pharmacy is near,
or if an eclipse will happen this year:

If I want to know the weather,
I must look out the window.

Spring is finally here in gradient warming trends;
the birds I do not hear are busy texting friends.

THIS IS

This is the third attempt,
neither sudden nor euphoric
but a researched, willful exercise
from which I hope to recover.

The words edited out of this poem
pile up knee deep on the floor
and rustle as I pace forth
then back through them.

If I don't survive the danger,
will companions notice
I am late, I am lost, or only
focus on my faults?

VACILANDO

"Not all who wander are lost."
—*Tolkien*

I
"Vacilando, *pres. part.* "Traveling when
the experience is more important
than the destination;
things that cannot translate well."

II
Perhaps I will never get there
but will travel just the same;
might be I never meet you,
but still call out your name.

In life there are some roses,
and there may be thorn attacks.
Sometimes it's all about romance;
sometimes it's just the facts.

WAKE UP

Waking up before the alarm
shoes and hat already on,
before the sun is up
I wash

Prepped before the day
begins, the kettle steaming,
two biscuits on a plate
to eat

Lightly on the treads descend;
slowly closing the door behind,
I turn to greet the chill winds
of March.

WAVES

Waves of pressure,
waves of light
I see you in the waves.

You look back amused
by the pettiness of my desire,
the inflexibility of my spine.

I see you in the waves,
so strong, magnetic,
you bend space and time,
cause my world to tilt.

I see you in the waves,
that must bear the weight
of each death and mother's cry
that seem so wrong and pointless.

I see you in the waves,
bright among the blessed stars
that challenge me in darkness
to also shine more bright.

Work with Hands

Have a craft that
makes hands callused;
if you whisper,
do so with passion.

What is the craft of words?
Take the line of words,
unravel from the spool,
weave them into useful fabric.

Tapestries of desire,
shrouds of meaning,
knit them into objects
of warmth and kindness.

Find some words
from your dusty past,
shine them up like new,
find out their worth.

CHANCE, RHYTHM, RHYME